A Penny on the Stair
and Other Poems

A Penny on the Stair and Other Poems

Flora Bolling Adams

BRANDYLANE PUBLISHERS
White Stone, Virginia

✻ Brandylane Publishers

P.O. Box 261, White Stone, Virginia 22578
(804) 435-6900 or 1 800 553-6922; e-mail: brandy@crosslink.net

Copyright 1998, by Flora Bolling Adams
All rights reserved
Printed in the United States of America

Library of Congress Cataloging-in-Publication Data

Adams, Flora Bolling, 1922–
   A penny on the stair and other poems/Flora Bolling Adams.
    p. cm.
   ISBN 1-883911-27-3
   I. Title
PS3551.D354P46 1998
811'.54—dc21   98–16332
                                                              CIP

This book is dedicated to all the children who have touched my heart with their delightful responses to the pleasant cadence of poetry.

Pretending   1
Thee (See)   1
The Wheelbarrow Ride   2
The Way I Like It   3
Let This Be Our Secret   4
A Sincere Compliment   4
Fair Is Fare   5
A Basket of Sweets   6
Consider This   6
In the Garden   7
To Mom, With Love   7
Dear Daddy   8
Now I Tell It, Dad   9
Learning on My Own Time   10
Please Stay   10
Thinking Back   11
Dear Mother   12
My Mother   12
A Change of Heart   13
My Bed   13
A Promise to Keep   14
Kelsey in the Evening   15
Exhilaration   16
Thoughts of a Veteran   17
An Invitation   18
A Crystal Bud Vase   19
A Penny on the Stair   20
Not Too Soon   21
Hurrah for Mother   21
Meadow Surprises   22
Window Shopping   23

Ben and the Squirrel   24
Betsy Barlowe   25
My Shadow   26
Humming Bird   27
A Very Special Someone   28
My Father's Eyes   29
The Message on a Card   30
Fun With Dad   31
She's Right   32
The Dentist   33
Horses   34
The Bumble Bee   35
Black Bird   36
Sorry   36
From Your Little Guy   37
Appreciation   37
Johnny Appleseed   38
The Bald Eagle   39
Army Ants   39
Preoccupied   40
Don't Be Late   41
A Teen   42
Wanting to Be Graceful   43
My House   44
Changing Weather   45
What Do We Do   46
I Will Not Share My Lollipops   47
To Young Passengers   48
Hypothetically Speaking   49
Brawny Tawny Anthony   50
Amoeba   51

The Sapper in the Minefield   52
Time   53
The Milky Way   53
The Desert   54
Gem Cutter   55
Alaska   56
The Man in the Kitchen   57
Whimsey   58
In the Ruin   59
Sleep Well   60
Seeking   61
The Silencing of the Insects   62
Osprey on the Outer Banks   63
Corolla's Shores   64
North Carolina's Outer Banks   65
Algonquin on Carrituck   66
Ants on a Vertical Straw   67
Poor Old Georgene   68
Wilma   69
Dream a New World of Peace   70
Thumbs   71
The Glove   72
Young Love   73
Defamation   74
For Lee   75
Hatred   76
Words   77
Who Am I?   78
A Message to My Child   79
The Ink Blot   80

Introduction

There is beauty and power in the spoken words of poetry. The melodic combinations, rhythm, and rhyme children love. Reading it once is not enough. Even children of ninety respond with a smile.

This small book of poems contains a variety reflecting a range of interests with little didacticism and moralizing. There are poems which express gratitude, poems which may shed a new and different light on well known things, poems about animals and nature, poems which tell a story, poems which reflect the sociological impact on young people, poems with humor and surprise endings, poems to add color and meaning to everyday experiences, poems to recite with special expressions, and poems about places and certain people and their jobs.

The first few pages are simple little verses. As we proceed up the staircase, the poems become a bit more involved.

Parents may see themselves in many of these poems. It is the author's hope that this group of saved poems will become shared reading and listening for the family.

Pretending

When I was just a little babe
You held me close to you.
That's why I hold my doll
Like this.
Now I'm a mommy, too.

Thee (See)

In cathe you think I'm changing
At too fatht a rate of thpeed
Wait until I thell you
A tooth ith what I need.
Today, a front one juth fell out;
You'll know it only when
I dethide to thing my thong
And thake a bow and grin.

The Wheelbarrow Ride

Pile in the straw and ride, ride, ride!
Samantha and Ray sit side by side.
Grand Dad pushes and away they go,
Sometimes fast and sometimes slow.
The red wheelbarrow is fun to ride,
Bumpety bump and side by side.

The Way I Like It

I love the way you do the things
That mothers always do.
The way you do them is unique:
You write, "From you know who!"
You wrap my sandwich different
From any other kid's.
The peanut butter on my bread
Has a thin sliced apple lid.

Let This Be Our Secret

Of all the teachers in the world,
You are my favorite girl.
Mom would be jealous if she knew
I love you, Miss McFurl.

A Sincere Compliment

Everyday is a picnic if I have you around.
A day with you
Is equal to
A day with my Bassett Hound.

Fair Is Fare

Of all the mothers in the world,
You are my special one.
Who else would tolerate the mess
I make when having fun!
But
One stipulation that you make
About eggs, when I beat them,
All mistakes are mine alone
And I, alone must eat them.
I don't add bananas any more.
I don't add vinegar any more.
I don't add peppermint any more.
I don't put in the shells anymore.
It's really not as much fun anymore.
I just beat them, heat them,
And then, I eat them!

A Basket of Sweets

Ruth brought me a basket of sweets
Tied up with a bow.
An assortment of family favorites,
But little did I know
That a great big bear or a great big lion
Was taking them one by one!
Watching them disappear so fast
Was one-sided fun.
So, to put a stop to all that theft,
Here is what I did:
I transferred what was left of them
And put them under lid!

Consider This

If you think I'm a problem
The way I talk to you,
You should hear the captain's parrot!
He is a sailor true.
He knows all the vernacular
And fluently squawks it;
He is definitely trilingual,
And talks and talks and talks it!

In the Garden

Violets, lilies, and buttercups
Border our garden walk,
The clumps of pansies dance and play
And nod when e're we talk;
But the dearest part of all I see
Is the bunny in the middle
Waiting till we walk away
So he can take a nibble.

To Mom, With Love

You have a sweet and loving smile
E'n when you're tired and blue.
When I get old I want to be
Exactly like you!

Dear Daddy,

Last night I dreamed a pleasant dream.
I wish that it were true.
I dreamed that you came home to stay
With me and Mommy too.
When you're with us a little while
You seem to get subdued;
You get restless; then you leave;
I think it's very rude
To leave us living all alone
And never drop us lines
To see how we are doing.
I get so sad sometimes.

Now I Tell It, Dad

The times you tucked me into bed
And tip-toed down the hall,
I always saw those creatures
Playing on the wall.
Sometimes they tumbled all about,
Turned round, and round, and round
Looking for me everywhere,
But I could not be found.
I scooted way down in the bed,
Got warmer and still hotter.
That's when I came up for some air
And cried for a drink of water!

Learning on My Own Time

I hope you will forgive me
For the things I fail to do;
I failed to put my games away.
And to do my homework, too.
When I came home, my games were out!
They kept me after classes
To do the work I failed to do!
How slowly recess passes!

Please Stay

It's not just the things you do for me
That makes me love you so;
It's the perfume of your presence.
Please, never, never go.

Thinking Back

I love when you are near me
And hum your happy tune.
The world seems bright and wonderful
And slips away too soon.
I still recall your watchful eye
With love in every glint,
Which was my time of childhood.
I wonder where it went!

Dear Mother

Mother's Day is a special time to tell you how I feel.
You are no longer with me, but my love for you is real.
Sometimes I think I should write to you
And then I know for sure
We have communed together;
Yes, angel thoughts are pure.

My Mother

You are a special mother
In every sort of way:
You know when I am real upset
Exactly what to say.
Soothing words and loving arms
From you, I can expect.
If voting for the Queen of Moms
It's you I would elect.
Life with you is golden,
A treasure in my heart;
I hope that we will never
Ever have to part.

A Change of Heart

Some kids seem to know a lot
Of this, that, and the other,
But no one ever explained to me
Why I got this baby brother.
I surely didn't want him
When they brought him home, you see.
But now, I hope we'll keep the kid;
Today, he smiled at me.

My Bed

I like to snuggle in my bed,
My blanket loosely o'er me lay,
Keeps me warm throughout the night
Lying on the sheets of white
Until the break of day.
My bed, my bed,
My cuddly, comfortable bed.

A Promise to Keep

A promise is a promise, Mom
And I'll keep mine to you.
How well I remember!
You kept your promise true.
You told me you would spank me
If I kept on bothering you.
That was in the theater;
The things a kid won't do!
I wanted all the popcorn and candy I could get.
And then, my thirst kept nagging me;
I can feel it even yet.
As daylight follows darkness,
I really had to go,
Down the aisle you jerked me,
Little did I know,
When we got home you'd do your job
And spank me, that's for certain.
You got a ruler about so wide
For me, I knew 'twas curtain.
But I tried to talk you out of it.
"I'll do what you command me,
Please try to think of some other way
That you can reprimand me."
I saw a grin show on your face
But your promise you would keep,
The rosey glow showed on my thighs
As I fell fast asleep.

Kelsey In the Evening

Long eye lashes curling, curling,
Framing eyes of glistening blue,
Not yet tired from pool and sunshine,
Exciting things still left to do.
Black hair tousled on the forehead,
Playing card games soon the goal,
Knit pajamas loosely fitting,
Eats rice pudding from a bowl.
Long eye lashes drooping, drooping,
Cheeks a healthy rosey red,
Gives up the day with loving kisses,
Climbs the stairs on up to bed.

Exhilaration

I watched an overgrown big tall teen
Put quarters in a coin machine
Which held an assortment of dogs and cats,
Stuffed and tumbled, this way and that
In a see-through cage with a plunging prong
That grabbed a toy and held it strong.
But sometimes the plunging prong just crashed.
That's when her little brother laughed and laughed
And laughed and laughed, and laughed and laughed;
Oh, how the little boy laughed!

Thoughts of a Veteran

When I was sent across the sea,
They issued weaponry to me
To fight a foreign war.
Some comrades died in battle strife;
I lost a limb, but not my life.
Sometimes I ask, "What for?"

An Invitation

Izzy lost a needle;
A favorite one of hers.
She's looked high,
She's looked low,
She's looked "everywheres."
It's a tiny, shiny needle
For stitches close together.
So come and help us find the thing,
No matter what the weather.
We'll look in a haystack
And try to find it then.
The date is May the first at one.
We'll eat, and talk, and grin!

A Crystal Bud Vase

For the last rose of summer
That you cut before the frost,
For a peony or hydrangea,
Or a bloom you like the most,
This little crystal bud vase
Can hold holly of December;
Even when it's empty,
Perhaps you will remember
The one who gave it to you
And tied it with a bow.
Much love is there within it,
As you and I both know.

A Penny on the Stair

I saw a penny on the stair
And didn't ask who dropped it there.
I passed it many times a day.
"It's just a penny," I would say.
I took my coin bag and went
To the Fireman's Circus in a big wide tent.
A man was doing tricks, you see;
Pointed a finger straight at me
and said,
"I have some change, here, in a heap,
If you can match it, it's yours to keep."
We counted the money and I'm sorry to report,
My pile of change was one penny short!

Not Too Soon

Remember when I was a tiny kid and didn't eat my beans?
Remember when I got bigger and slashed my new blue jeans?
I've learned an awful lot since then.
I do the things I oughta;
I'm filling up my piggy bank
With every dime and quartah
To get the kids the things they need
For school and winter weather.
I'm taking many short-cuts:
I seldom buy them leather.
Even though I'm fairly young,
I'm smart enough to know
That slashes in designer jeans
Just grow and grow and grow.

Hurrah for Mother

Of all the gifts God gave to me,
There's none one way or other
That can compare to the gift I got
When you became my mother.

Meadow Surprises

Let us walk to our meadow
To see who is playing there.
Could it be nymphs and fairies
Climbing a golden stair?
Or, could it be a monarch butterfly,
Or a viceroy on the wing,
To show their beautiful colors
While the male cicadas sing?
Who can it be in our meadow
Laughing and playing today?
Is it a prospect of friendship?
A wish come true in May?

Window Shopping

Why is it, when we go window shopping
We don't buy windows?
We just look at this and that!
Shelly likes to look at toys.
Suzan looks at big straw hats.
Nance just wants to look at boys;
Bailey looks at balls and bats.
Father looks at tools and gadgets,
Mother looks at silks and such.
The shops are closed and we can't purchase;
I don't like window shopping much.

Ben and the Squirrel

Ben put some corn out on a nail
And waited patiently to see
The squirrel come scampering along
And gnaw the grain off, hungrily.
He stopped to fix a little lunch
For Bea and Beau and Bob.
All he saw when he looked again
Was a big red empty cob!

Betsy Barlowe

Little Betsy Barlowe
Loves her nursery rhymes;
When her mother reads to her
She dances and she mimes.

When Betsy plays alone
Or goes with Mom to shop,
She chants what she remembers
Twirling like a top.

One, two, buckle my shoe,
Three, eight, pick up sticks,
Seven, nine, lay them straight!
Five, six, big fat hen!

Little Betsy Barlowe
Can count as you can see;
But not always in sequence;
She will when she is three.

My Shadow

My shadow is an ethereal thing
That hides when day is done.
It is always a part of me
From dawn to setting sun.
It trails behind me mornings;
Past noon it leads the way.
When I am standing on it,
I know it is mid-day.
On cloudy days, my shadow
Won't go along with me.
But when the sun shines brightly,
It keeps me company.

Humming Bird

A tiny bundle of flutter
Hovering by a bloom,
Flitting all around the bower,
Sipping nectar from a flower,
Smells its sweet perfume.
A tiny bundle of flutter
With bill and radiant plume
Zips left and right, so fast in flight,
How quickly it can zoom
To intimidate another bird
That's come to taste and drink
Of nature's bounty and supply
Entwined upon the trellis high!
A show to watch, I think!
But the most amusing part to me,
He bothers not the bumble bee!

A Very Special Someone

When I'm a full-grown person
I hope I'm just like you.
I like the way you sing and dance
And cook lasagna too.
You're always calm and cheerful
When friends come by to play.
You are the same, kind person
Today and every day.

My Father's Eyes

My father's eyes are greenish gray,
Sometimes, a grayish blue;
It seems they change their colors
By the various things I do.
But when he looks at me and winks,
I have no fear of what he thinks.

The Message on a Card

Mother Dear, you're easy to love
Because you're good and kind.
I'm glad you chose me for your own
To love and keep and mind.
My need you met and I filled yours;
Your need to be a mother,
I am your child, your only child
Who loves you as no other.

Fun With Dad

Remember last vacation time, our auto had a flat?
And Dad said, "Gilly, Golly, what do you think of that?
    Just when you have to change the tire
      Your mind is all a muddle."
And then he saw that he had stopped:
    In a muddy roadside puddle.
He fixed the flat and then he laughed,
    "This time I've really got 'em!
    But why, oh why, is every flat
      Always on the bottom?"

She's Right

In my big rush each morning when
I leave home for school,
I think about the put-downs
And all the ridicule
I get from some kids on the block
While waiting for the bus.
My mother says, "Ignore them, Dear.
They do not speak for us!"

The Dentist

The dentist has a little room
With a great chair in the middle,
And a tall stool that he sits on
When he tells a joke or riddle.
He pokes around all in my mouth
And makes me open wide
So he can see what's lurking
Way down deep inside.
The drill goes zing and he fills a tooth,
And tells me how to rinse.
It's been at least a year or two.
I haven't been back since.
Mom says I need a check-up now;
I'll go without a tear
To see that little fountain
That gurgled by my ear.

Horses

My heart leaps up
Whenever I see
Horses in the meadow
Running wild and free.

No bits between their teeth,
No riders on their backs,
Nothing whatever to halter them,
Nor loaded down with packs.

Freedom for the horses!
Sleek as they can be!
Grazing in the meadow,
That's what I like to see.

Horses' tails a-switching,
Grass up to the knee,
Harmony in the meadow,
Equine ecstasy.

The Bumble Bee

The bee that bumbles is the Bumble Bee.
He bores little holes in the apple tree.
The wings of his are too small for his size
But he doesn't know it and away he flies.
Little short flights, he bumbles along
Buzzing his angry Bumble Bee Song.

Black Bird

Black bird, Black bird,
Sailing on high
Around in circles
Slicing the sky.

Black bird, Black bird,
How do you know
A creature is dying
Down here below?

Wide winged black bird,
You prey as you do.
The world needs scavengers
Such as you.

Sorry

I'm sorry I made you worry
When I stayed gone too long.
But I didn't want the curfew
To interrupt my song.

From Your Little Guy

It's too bad all boys and girls
Don't have a mom like you.
You know how I hate my curls,
Eyelashes and dimples, too.
Why I have them, I don't know,
I'd trade them if I could.
The starch I used turned into dough!
You told me that it would.
I'm glad you understood, Mom,
When my lashes I had trimmed.
But they just grew longer, Mom.
You bought a hat wide brimmed
For me to wear to hide my curls
And shades to help me see.
You don't tease like all the girls
That BALD's the way to be!

Appreciation

Of all the things you give me, Dad,
I treasure most your love;
Your heart is pure. You're wonderful.
True as the stars above.
If we were rich, would we ever
Know how to live as we do?
The gladness that I feel each day
Is all because of you.

Johnny Appleseed

"Oh, Johnny, Johnny, Johnny Appleseed
Where do you like to roam?"
"I follow my nose wherever it takes me.
Any place I can call home.
Log cabins await me along the wide stretches
From the Ohio to the northern lakes.
I plant the appleseeds I get from cider mills
And I have no fear of snakes."

"Oh, Johnny, Johnny, Johnny Appleseed,
We thank you for the orchard nearby!
We eat the Jonathan, the Yellow Transparent,
And also, the Northern Spy.
Come sit by our fire place
And eat some wild turkey
And tell us the latest news.
Why you are barefoot, cold winds must chill you."

"My ways are the ways I choose.
I go barefoot to save my shoe leather.
I tramp to where soil is good loam.
I plant the seeds and pile brush around them.
The frontier is always my home."

The Bald Eagle

Along the Chilkat River
Where salmon like to run
Bald eagles gather every year
To eat and feed their young.

The Chilkat River is a favorite place,
The salmon think, it's nice;
Warm water wells up from the shore
And keeps it free of ice.

The eagles fly.
The salmon swim.
The salmon lose;
The eagles win.

Army Ants

I don't know much about Army Ants;
But I could learn, if I had a chance.
Dad says they're vicious as can be,
Since I don't want them chewing on me,
I'll just read about them,
Yes Siree!

Preoccupied

"Daddy, may I open this?
Say, Daddy, huh?
I can't do it myself, can I?
Say, Daddy, huh?"

"Just a minute, Buddy,
Just a minute."

"Hey, Daddy, please show me how this works.
It looks like fun."

"Just a minute Buddy,"
(The trouble has begun.)

"Daddy, Daddy, is this a toy?
For a little boy?
Daddy, Daddy,"

"What did you say Buddy?
Where did you get that?
You must always ask Daddy!"

Don't Be Late

There are times never to be late.
Just think, and you will know
How inconsiderate it is
To interrupt the show.
Your grand entrance won't be announced.
So come early and you can see
The beginning of the program,
And cheer most neighborly.

A Teen

I am just a teenager
And what do I know?
I know quite a lot
But not how to go.
The models and patterns
Give me little to choose.
If I don't get it right
I'm the one who will lose.
So, how shall I go?
The road is a maze.
My life is in a balance
Of confusion and haze.

Wanting To Be Graceful

You're as graceful as a swan
Upon the lake in May.
Why am I so awkward
In every kind of way?
When I walk, I stumble
Over my big shoes.
My arms and legs are longer;
I always get the blues!
It seems I've grown a foot or two
Since I learned that dance
You and I were doing.
I hope I get the chance
To dance with you another time
When I get used to me.
Perhaps I can be graceful, too.
We'll have to wait and see.

My House

I'll build my house upon a rock,
Not on the sinking sand.
I'll build it on a rise, for sure,
So I can view the land
Where floods will not be beating
And coming in my door.
I'll leave the space that waters need,
And they won't ask for more.

Changing Weather

Dark clouds are in the northern sky.
The wind is tossing leaves on high.
The trees are waving limbs about;
Shirts on the line are rounded out.
Bright October too soon has passed;
November's here with winter blast.
Logs in the fireplace glow with heat;
The rocking chair with cushion seat
And footstool ready for the feet
There by the chimney wall together,
Denote the sudden change in weather.
Soup's in the pot, ready to eat;
The family comes with hurried feet,
Sit down for a tasty treat.
A day like this just can't be beat!

What Do We Do

What do we do when it snows on Sunday,
The streets are slick, no school on Monday?

What do we do when it snows all night,
Piles up high, no stop in sight?

We sit by the fire while the morning passes,
Roast potatoes in a pile of ashes,

Read a book or magazine,
Repair a coat on the stitch machine,

Dress up warm from head to toe,
Go outside to play in the snow.

Mama with the saucer, Dad with the sled
Pull us kids past the old toolshed

To the field with not a fence post in it.
Away we slide in half a minute!

Down we zoom on saucer and sled!
Wind blows hard, our noses red.

That's what we do when it snows on Sunday
And streets are bad, no school on Monday!

I Will Not Share My Lollipops

I will not share my lollipops!
So what, if I have two?
Just because you're my sister
Do I need give one to you?
I know we both like lemon and lime;
We are so alike that way;
Last night you tasted my dessert,
And also my entrée.
I realize I'm older
And with me you like to lounge;
I've no problem with your wearing
All my hand-me-downs.
So, please, please, little sister,
Please don't be a pest!
Don't mess around and drool about
My things I like the best!
Your inactivity gets to me!
I think you're getting fat!
Why don't you run on out and play
And not be such a brat?

That's how I felt some months ago.
It's different now, for sure.
The doctor says she's very sick.
I hope she can endure
The surgery on her kidneys.
Please tell her, Mom, for me
That I will give her one of mine,
Since I have two, you see.

To Young Passengers

When Mommy drives and traffic bears heavy
On her attention, she must watch with care,
Be defensive to protect her family
Riding in comfort with no distress to bear.
The highway might be wet and slick with oil
In places she must brake to slack her speed.
A petty dispute between two siblings
Is distraction that she surely does not need!
"Do not hit!
Do not slap!
Do not quarrel!"
Your calmness will be helpful all the way.
Your ride will be safer and more lovely.
If perchance you can hear and heed her say.
Your trip, more surely will be a pleasure;
Your life, safely borne, will be your treasure.

Hypothetically Speaking

If you were going to be a shoe,
What kind of shoe would you be?
Would you be a sandal?
An open-toe pump?
Or a boot that zips to the knee?
Would you have buckles?
High heels and straps?
Would you be dainty for dress?
Would you be popular?
Stylish to wear?
Expensive, more or less?

If I were going to be a shoe,
A substantial one I'd be.
I would be genuine, inside and out
And smiles would shine on me.
I would be dependable,
Of classic design;
My attributes humanly cast.
I would be tanned and fashioned with love.
My sole would be made to last.
My mate would mirror my perfection.
A pair we would always be.
We would walk in harmony together
And serve humanity.

Brawny Tawny Anthony

Brawny Tawny Anthony high up in a tree,
Sawing limbs from a mighty oak,
Saw dust flying free.
Sitting on a leather strap, his seat up in the air,
His feet are shod with graspers
That hold him safely there.
The strap that hugs the mighty oak lets his hands go free
So he can hold the chain saw and delimb the mighty tree.
The buckers stationed on the ground saw the limbs apart
And pile the future fire wood
To sell. That shows they're smart!
Brawny Tawny Anthony climbs higher and peers around
To figure out how he'll protect
The shrubbery on the ground.
The saw goes zing and sings its song.
His muscles firm and taut,
He tops the tree and lets it land
Exactly where he thought.
He made a calculation and well it was indeed
Of how much more to shorten the tree,
And the felling space he'd need.
He shimmied down the limb-stripped oak,
And wiped his sweaty brow;
As he stretched and exercised his legs
Said, "I want a drink, right now!"
The buckers piled the big logs and made a felling bed
To protect the owner's driveway,
The way Boss Frazier said.
Anthony took the chain saw, with an undercut he made it:
A wedge-shaped piece close to the ground,
On the bed of logs he laid it.
Brawny Tawny Anthony, skillful as can be,
Respects the danger in his job
And works so carefully.

Amoeba

The amoeba, a one-celled animal,
Is too small to even see,
Except under a microscope.
How strange its life must be!
The way it moves about and eats
Elusive as can be,
Changing shapes and engulfing
Some smaller thing than he
Is very, very interesting.
I watched it all through class.
I did not keep a record
Of what I did, alas!
My experiment was incomplete.
Next time, I have a mission.
I'll record how they multiply;
They divide! That is, by fission.
Don't you think the amoeba
Is quite a mathematician?

The Sapper in the Minefield

The sapper, silent in his tread,
Makes no casual movements
Through treacherous minefields.
His clarity of mind directs his cautious fingers,
As he traces a complex arrangement of wires.
Each move deliberate and calculated,
To defuse, he holds his breath,
Never looking past the danger,
Snips at a selected place,
And dismantles a hunk of devastation.
His luck holds once more!
He exhales the long-held breath.
Within his soul there is light; there is music,
The sheer exhilaration of success!

Time

What is Time?
It's hard to guess it,
But the work of an inch worm can express it.
This is the way it seems to me:
He measures off segments of eternity.

The Milky Way

Today I saw the Milky Way,
Just like the arch on a starry night.
Motes of dust were turning, dancing,
Shining brightly in a ray of light.

The Desert

The desert is a land of rock and sand;
It seldom rains there, I hear.
The sun shines down and bakes the land;
It's hot and dry all year.

Who wants to live in a place like that?
There are some creatures that really do.
They have adapted to the habitat;
There's plants that live there too.

All living things need a place to be,
Where they can be safe from harm;
With plenty of food a reality,
The desert, for some, has charm.

The badger and the pocket mouse
Have burrows under the ground.
The pack rat keeps a messy house
With litter she has found.

The tortoise and the horned toad
Have very little to fear;
Their armor seems a heavy load,
But keeps them safe all year;

The cactus has prickles all over it;
So it is self-protected.
When all the animals discover it,
It's the desert plant rejected.

The desert seems to be a barren ground;
The nights are breezy and cold.
Dew forms in droplets all around.
All life drinks up what can be found,
More precious than pure gold!

Gem Cutter

The gem cutter, in his game of secrets,
Deliberate in every cut,
Looks not back from the present moment.
Each slice reveals new wonders,
A descant from the ages,
A universe of jewels!
And he chisels on.

Alaska

Alaska is the largest state
In all the U.S. A.
Texas used to make that claim
That, no more she can say.
Alaska is twice Texas' size;
She joined the union late;
In '59, she became a part
Of the "lower forty-eight."

Alaska, close to Asia,
Across the Berring Strait,
Was known as Seward's Ice Box,
Not held a purchase great.
About two cents an acre!
What would it cost today?
All the fish and minerals
Worth more than we could pay.

Seward was a wise man.
Russia is no way proud.
That she sold us Big Alaska,
A land so well endowed.

The Man In The Kitchen

Why are all the cabinets open
In the kitchen this fine day?
The Man is in the cook room,
So, don't get in his way!
Don't close the refrigerator door!
Don't turn a burner down!
Don't turn off the hot water
That is steaming all around!
Wet eggs in the carton give him no alarm;
The unused sausage on the tray
Is soft and limp and warm.
Everything is on the counter!
Please don't get me wrong.
Warm plates are waiting to be filled.
The coffee's hot and strong.
The eggs are fixed to perfection;
Your preference you must tell:
Coddled, poached, or scrambled,
Or boiled in the shell,
Overlight, or sunnyside up,
To him it's a disgrace
To serve an egg that has a fringe
Of curly, fried, brown lace.
The apples are scorched to "just right"
The jam is in the jar.
To get a better breakfast,
You'd have to go quite far.
The bagels and the buttered toast
Have not a tinge of char.

Whimsey

Come along with me and I will show you
Something you must see down at the rill.
The spring that bubbles up from the embankment
Does more than merely trickle down the hill.

A little boy has built a water wheel,
From scraps of shingles trimmed to suit his need.
When you get near, you'll hear its rhythm
And remember all about it, yes indeed.

He used a cast-off piece of copper pipe
To bring the water to an even stream;
And set the wheel precisely beneath it.
Ingenuity of our brother Gene!

Years and years ago was when he made it.
How could it last so long? What is the cause?
Every spring the road is scraped and levelled,
And roadmen put it back the way it was.

They recall the time when they were children
And played to try to make their dreams so real.
The whimsey, the quaint, and the fanciful,
Merry splatter of water on the wheel.

In the Ruin

Night falls fast,
Filling up the ruin.
A damaged, sacred statue,
A lone sentinel,
Says nothing,
Speaks volumes,
And grieves alone.

Sleep Well

Sleep well, my friend;
The circumstances around you do not keep you wide-eyed.
But your attitude which is there within you, does!
Let the light of Divine Countenance
Cover you, like a blanket.
And sleep well.

Seeking

How can I enjoy life?
How can I know what's right?
How can I know which way to go
And say what will enlight?
I need to be on my merry way
And decide what I should pursue!
So, tell me, My Muse without being abstruse,
Just what am I meant to do?

"Begin each day with a poem.
End each day with a song.
To yourself, always be true
In everything you choose to do,
Then, you will do no wrong."

The Silencing of the Insects

The lusty choir, the chorale, and symphony
In the forest every day is never heard
By the millions of people on the highways,
In the homes, in the byways,
Neither do they hear the song of bird.
What do they hear?
The hum of motors, the honking of horns,
The screeching of brakes each night and morn,
The roar of the air plane up in the sky,
Or a helicopter flying by,
The sounds of the train upon the track,
The lonesome whistle, the clickety-clack.
All sounds of transport;
The din of the city,
The clamor and uproar,
Oh, what a pity
That we never can hear
The songs of the insects
Living so near!

Osprey on the Outer Banks

Osprey all along the Outer Banks in early spring
Have a mission:
To build a nest, lay the eggs,
Hatch, and raise their young.
And then, at the right time for them,
Return to Brazil;
There, to fulfill a repeat mission.
Oh, that the young of man
Should at birth, inherently know
All that man knows
About existence
As the young of birds
Instinctively know
The ways of their kind!

Corolla's Shores

Along Corolla's lonely shores of old
Where no lighthouse ever was
There is a watery bed where ships
Sunken in the cool, dark deep
Lie still and moldering.
Wild Spanish horses, free to roam
For centuries, smell the old wrecks
On the sand dunes and from this rise
Gaze into the sea
As though they sense that some time in the past
They swam from a shipwreck
To safety, on Corolla.

North Carolina's Outer Banks

Outer Banks,
Barrier Islands—
Dynamic stretching strips of shifting sand
Along the Atlantic Coast
Laugh with the Sea;
At man's attempts to stabilize them.
Powerful is their natural inclination
To join the mainland to the West!

Algonquin on Carrituck

Algonquin on Carrituck, searching, hunting,
Gathering from the sea's bounty
Fish, slick and scaly, fresh
Oysters tightly clamped
Protecting their quickening and treasure;
Clams, the subsistence of a hardy people
Able, willing to adjust
To the shifting, shifting, always shifting sands:
The sea's powerful kneading,
Here a little, there a little
Makes the slow, constant change which
Disturbs not the Algonquin who persevere
In a fragile milieu where no landmarks
Exist over time.
Only the sea makes a marked disturbance
Of the universe.

Ants on A Vertical Straw

Ants are crawling up a straw;
Their ladder of life—and time goes by!
Social insects with a purpose,
But like all creatures
They must die.
When they reach the tip-top segment
No more noses can they touch;
There, they drop beyond life's milieu
Where cares of ants don't matter much.
If you watch them, you will notice,
Some of them won't go up high.
Around the middle they try to linger,
No one told me, but I know why.

Poor Old Georgene

Like ladies on the silver screen
And in the fashion magazine
Who wore their brows arched high and thin
With plastered face and hungered mien,
That group Georgene would be in!
Poor old Georgene, when she was just thirteen,
Plucked her brows away back then,
But none grew back where those had been.

Wilma

Who is Wilma?
What is she,
That all her friends commend her?
Wilma is The Lady Extraordinaire.
Her tongue speaks
Only after her thoughts have been tempered
And sifted
Through her sieve of careful consideration.
If you ask her for advice,
You will do well to take it;
There will be no ulterior motive
In the response from her heart,
Because that great heart of hers
Exudes much love.

Dream A New World of Peace

A good man had a dream.
A dream of a different kind of world.
Can we dream a New World into reality?
If it's from the purity of our hearts!
Perceive it, know it, understand it, live it.
And the New World of peace and harmony,
That sacred consciousness of Love,
The leaven that enlarges the whole lump
Will abide in the hearts of the children of all nations.
And we shall know Peace.
Peace, glorious Peace.

Thumbs

In symmetrical balance, two digits
Define the nature of mankind,
As do the eyes, the ears, and the nostrils,
The perfect expression of Mind.

Chromosomes denote the human species.
One less could not create a human hand
That can grasp a bar, a tool, a pencil.
Of all Primata, the human's in command.

If they're down, it's no, no, no!
If they're out, it's go, go, go!
If you're awkward, you're all of them.
If you're a gardener, the leaf and stem
Will be the same color as old five on your hand
And you are known as tiller of the land.

They help you to pick up a pin from the floor,
To thread a needle and much, much more.
Enclosing the fingers into a fist
The hand becomes a weapon attached to the wrist.
Unfold it to use it; be upright and kind.
The Thumbs of Man is an expression of Mind.

The Glove

A leather glove is in my drawer;
No sense of life within its fold;
It speaks to me of loneliness
And faints away within my hold.
It is as I, and it is mine;
There is communion here, divine.
Its sense of loss does not abate;
I tell it I, too, miss my mate.

Young Love

Young Love, like the bud of a wild rose, is
Closed tightly in the heart, yet to unfold;
The lively spark that's sealed within the swell
Will glow to an effulgence to behold.
Young Love is but a fragile, tender sprout
That peaks up through the earth in early spring;
Its dormancy no longer keeps its slumber,
A freshness to the heart its growth will bring.
Young Love is a frail and fragile tendril.
On brittle stalk it clings with fragrance rare;
Its dewy leaves glisten in briolettes
Like teardrops on the cheeks of maiden fair.
Young Love blooms and always keeps its fragrance
Far into fall and winter's snow-white hair.

Defamation

Renown family, generally upright
With innermost desires for privacy
In their world of fortune and politics
Suffer.
One bungle by one member,
A slip of the tongue
Or an act of poor judgment
Exploited by the Tabloid Press
Becomes an explosion of rumor and innuendo
Meant to malign the motives and integrity
Of the entire family.
The half truths, the lies, the slander
Left floating on the airwaves,
Never to be unsaid,
Defame and injure the young ones
Whose lives must be extra circumspect
To regain the original family respect,
To stay in the fold of structure and integrity.

For Lee

Look to the mountains!
Look to the skies!
There are colors of every hue.
But for stars, you must look
Into Gerry's eyes,
Jewels of delphinium blue.
Oh blue, blue,
Delphinium blue!
The waters reflect the skies;
But for the love,
That true, pure love,
Just look into Gerry's eyes.

Hatred

Hate no man of God's creation;
Hate yields sickness, sin, and sorrow;
Hatred's cold, it has no blessings,
Lines the face with vile expression;
Anger is the vent for hatred;
Darts of madness, wounds inflicting.
Who is man that you should hate him?
Hate him with an evil vengeance?
Could you hate God's own creation?
Hate his own reflected image?
Pray that you release the hatred
Gripping life with its compulsion.
Loving thoughts about your neighbor
Harbor no ill will, but blessings.
Love will change the wanton hatred;
Love will heal the wounds of vengeance;
Love is Light, it knows no darkness.
Man is altogether lovely,
If perceived with understanding.
God intended man to love Him;
Love each other as true brothers.

Words

Words, words, words,
Sometimes I think about words.
Their rhythm.
Some words like cricket, gurgle, promiscuity,
Jump and run along
Like a shallow stream over rounded stones and pebbles.
Others, like nightingale, pillow, molasses, loiter about;
No motivation at all.
Some words are fast:
Ship, heat, misty, seem, picnic;
Some are slow:
Cool, stretch, roll, moral, curl;
I like curl.
It can be a tight spiral,
A strand that relaxes
Into a comfortable wave;
It can be a kitten asleep.
Curl is comfort, in no hurry.
I like words.
Some words sound the same
But have different meanings,
And different spellings.
Sometimes the same word
Means different things.
It depends on where it is located
In the sentence:
"I saw a saw in the shop when we went to shop."
Understand?
Words, words, words!
I like words!

Who Am I?

I am a reflection
Of what I think,
What I feel.
I am an ever-flowing,
Always-changing river,
A channel of compassion,
Of trust, truth, and forgiveness.
Progressing, progressing, progressing.
I cannot go back!
My way is clear
In the ever-present, perfect Now.

A Message to My Child

Live rightly today,
Then every yesterday
Will have no taint of remorse;
Every tomorrow will be
A rainbow of glorious expectations.
And My Darling, if you do not receive
A present reward, examine your interpretation
Of the events,
For there is indeed a blessing in each effort.

The Ink Blot

The splash of ink upon the page
Holds information infinite.
The seer sees the message clear,
Then dips the pen into the smear,
And writes the lines, most definite.

First Lines

Alaska is the largest state   *56*
Algonquin on Carrituck, searching, hunting   *66*
Along Corolla's lonely shores of old   *64*
Along the Chilkat River   *39*
Ants are crawling up a straw   *67*
A good man had a dream   *70*
A leather glove is in my drawer   *72*
A promise is a promise, Mom   *14*
A tiny bundle of flutter   *27*
Ben put some corn out on a nail   *24*
Black bird, Black bird   *36*
Brawny, tawny Anthony high up in a tree   *50*
Come along with me and I will show you   *58*
Daddy, may I open this?   *40*
Dark clouds are in the northern sky   *45*
Every day is a picnic if I have you around   *4*
For the last rose of summer   *19*
Hate no man of God's creation   *76*
How can I enjoy life?   *61*
I am a reflection   *78*
I am just a teenager   *42*
I don't know much about Army Ants   *39*
I hope you will forgive me   *10*
I like to snuggle in my bed   *13*
I love the way you do the things   *3*
I love when you are near me   *11*
If you think I'm a problem   *6*
If you were going to be a shoe   *49*
I'll build my house upon a rock   *44*
I'm sorry I made you worry   *36*
In cathe you think I'm changing   *1*
In my big rush each morning when—   *32*
In symmetrical balance, two digits   *71*

81

It's not just the things you do for me   10
It's too bad all boys and girls   37
I saw a penny on the stair   20
I watched an overgrown big tall teen   16
I will not share my lollipops   47
Izzy lost a needle   18
Last night I dreamed a pleasant dream   8
Let us walk to our meadow   22
Like ladies on the silver screen   68
Little Betsy Barlowe   25
Live rightly today   79
Long eye lashes curling, curling   15
Look to the mountains   75
Mother's Day is a special time to   12
Mother Dear, you are easy to love   30
My father's eyes are a greenish gray   29
My heart leaps up   34
My shadow is an ethereal thing   26
Night falls fast   59
Of all the gifts God gave to me   21
Of all the mothers in the world   5
Of all the teachers in the world   4
Of all the things you give me, Dad   37
Oh, Johnny, Johnny, Johnny Appleseed   38
Osprey all along the Outer Banks in early spring   63
Outer Banks, Barrier Islands   65
Pile in the straw and we'll ride, ride, ride   2
Renown family, generally upright   74
Remember last vacation time, our auto had a flat?   31
Remember when I was a tiny kid and didn't eat my beans?   21
Ruth brought me a basket of sweets   6
Sleep well, my friend   60
Some kids seem to know a lot   13
The amoeba, a one-celled animal   51
The bee that bumbles is the Bumble Bee   35

The dentist has a little room   *33*
The desert is a land of rock and sand   *54*
The gem cutter, in his game of secrets   *55*
The lusty choir, the chorale, and symphony   *62*
The sapper, silent in his tread   *52*
The splash of ink upon the page   *80*
The times you tucked me into bed   *9*
There are times never to be late   *41*
Today I saw the Milky Way   *53*
Violets, lilies and buttercups   *7*
What do we do when it snows on Sunday?   *46*
What is Time?   *53*
When I'm a full-grown person   *28*
When I was just a little babe   *1*
When I was sent across the sea   *17*
When Mommy drives and traffic bears heavy   *48*
Who is Wilma?   *69*
Why are all the cabinets open—?   *57*
Why is it, when we go window shopping—?   *23*
Words, words, words   *77*
You are a special mother   *12*
You have a sweet and loving smile   *7*
Young Love, like the bud of a wild rose, is   *73*
You're as graceful as a swan   *43*

Born in Flat Gap, Virginia, Flora Bolling Adams was the ninth of eleven children. She graduated from the University of Maryland with B.S. and M.Ed. degrees, and is a retired teacher of reading and language arts. Primarily in Montgomery County, Maryland, she taught elementary school, developed curricula in health, language arts and social studies for K-12, and taught in-service courses in a variety of subject areas. She and her husband Kelsey have four children and six grandchildren. Mrs. Adams's play, *The U.S. Constitution*, was published by Norton Press, and her story, *Tank Hill* is scheduled for release in 1998 by Sovereign Publishers. She lives and writes in Williamsburg, Virginia.

Cover art and interior pen and ink drawings are by David Narvaez, an artist and sculptor who lives in Virginia's Middle Peninsula. Mr. Narvaez also illustrated Mrs. Adams's book, *Tank Hill*.